Remote Control is a real eye— for
teachers, parents, and youth wo— uth
think clearly through the mudd—
— Sean Mc
Author and conference speaker

One of the major challenges facing Christians today is the morally challenged influence the media has on our teenagers. At the Summit, we educate the next generation of Christian young people to have a biblical Christian world view. Our prayer is that this education will equip them to dive into the culture with eyes wide open and indeed make a positive impact on the culture. *Remote Control* is a book that is going to help open the eyes of the Christian community to the world's hidden agenda that is found in movies, TV, press, comics, etc. Until Christians become aware of the tools the world is using to undermine their biblical world view, we will never be effective in communicating the gospel message to this media-saturated culture. Carl's book will help teens and parents find creative ways to open up conversations with their families and friends, those who are lost or searching, and talk about what is really important — God's point of view which impacts the culture toward the good, the true, and the beautiful.
— David A. Noebel
Summit Ministries

Carl Kerby has made me more aware of how this culture is getting away from the Bible and its teachings. After hearing Carl speak on pop culture and how evolution is getting into the main-stream culture in even subtle ways, I started to recognize this my-self. Even last week, while watching the race-car movie *Talladega Nights*, I was shocked to hear a line regarding evolution. Carl has helped teach me to think critically about what is happening in our culture.
— Teri MacDonald
Professional race car driver
Driven to Dream Ministries.org

Most of us have no idea that popular TV programs, movies, and books for children often contain material that serves to indoctrinate them in evolution. In this book, Carl Kerby describes numerous examples in popular TV programs and movies that, while they were truly funny and entertaining, especially to children, included dialogue which openly or subtly promoted evolution as fact. Unless parents are aware and prepared to explain the truth of God's creation when their children are exposed to such false notions, children may absorb teachings in early childhood that they will carry into later life. You will find it not only informative but entertaining. I highly recommend it to parents.

> — Duane T. Gish
> The Institute for Creation Research

If you've ever wondered how deeply ingrained evolutionary thinking has become in our society, wonder no more. Carl Kerby has done a masterful job in focusing attention on the evolutionary undertones of innocents from *Spider-Man* to *CSI*. This book will open your eyes to things you need to detect in order to think and live biblically.

> — Dr. Woodrow Kroll,
> President, Back to the Bible International

Did you know that false evolutionary teaching can creep into your thinking in some very unexpected ways? Carl Kerby takes a look at this subject in *Remote Control*. It is loaded with fascinating examples of how the father of lies has placed the lies of evolution right in front of us in the media so we will trip and fall and believe that world view. What is the solution? Read your Bible and obey what you read. God's holy Word has stood the test of time. Evolution will fall into the dust bins of history as another false teaching and God's Word and Jesus Christ will not. Time is short, so make your choice on what world view you are going to put eternal trust into.

> — Mark Cahill
> Founder, Mark Cahill Ministries

Remote Control by Carl Kerby will be an eye-opening shock to many parents as they learn of the subtle-but-powerful influences of movies and television programs that indoctrinate children and adults in evolutionary ideas. This book is must reading for all Christian families to learn to use "biblical radar" to discern and counter the secular influences of Hollywood.

> — Ken Ham,
> President, Answers in Genesis, USA

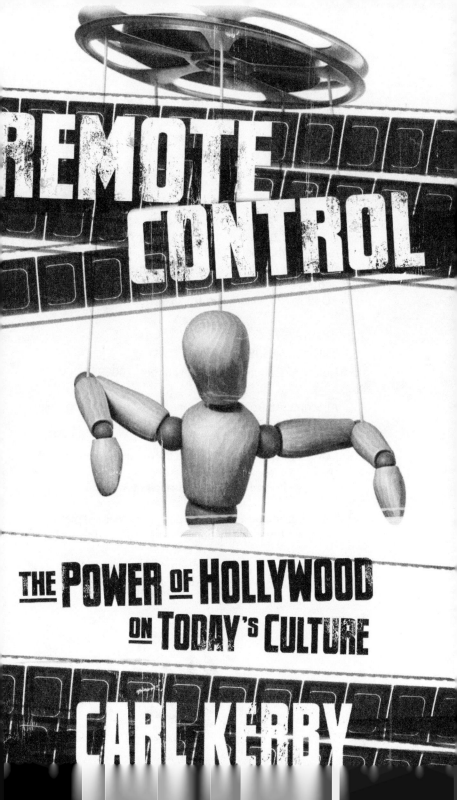

First Printing: October 2006

ISBN-13: 978-0-89051-491-7
ISBN-10: 0-89051-491-7
Library of Congress Catalog Number: 2006934885

All Scripture is from the New King James Version of the Bible, unless otherwise noted.

Cover by Jayme Brandt, Twice Born, Eureka Springs, AR.

Printed in the United States of America.

For information regarding author interviews, please contact the publicity department at (870) 438-5288.

Please visit our website for other great titles:
www.masterbooks.net.

Master
Books

A Division of New Leaf Publishing Group

Acknowledgments

This book would never have happened without Master Books. Thanks, guys, for all your support and work. I know the Master Books team put in a lot of effort to take my talk on this subject and turn it into a book. You're the best!

Masami, you are the greatest gift, apart from salvation, that Jesus Christ has given to me. I know I drive you crazy with all the travel. Thanks for putting up with me for all these years. I love you very much and look forward to what God has in store for us for many years to come.

Alisa and Dennis. This book is a direct result of our efforts to raise godly children. No doubt, I failed many times and will fail many more as a parent. In spite of that, I do love you guys, a lot!

Alisa, I apologize for *The Fly*! Hey, I wasn't saved then! God has blessed you in spite of that experience. Thanks for showing me grace.

Dennis, I can't wait to watch more of your creations. Please keep making movies and documentaries focused on Christ!

Praise God that in spite of our failures you guys are a real blessing. Stay strong in your faith and service to the Lord!

Woodrow Kroll and Art Figurski, I'll always be thankful to you and your wives for praying with and for me in Branson. That was a time that really fully confirmed in my mind that God was calling Masami and me into full-time, vocational ministry. You guys hold a very special place in my heart. May God continue to bless *Back to the Bible* through your humble service.

Mark Cahill, I love you man! It is always a huge encouragement to me when we speak. Hearing how the Lord is constantly using you to share the gospel with so many people challenges me to step up and share my faith even more. Thank you, my friend!

Last, but definitely not least, Ken Ham. Ken, thank you! I can't believe that you would allow a guy like me to be involved in ministry with you. It is hard for me to understand how you would — even though I know you took some heat — let a former air traffic controller, the son of a professional wrestler, speak on behalf of the ministry that God has built around you. Your book *The Lie* impacted me so strongly, my life has not been the same since reading it. I appreciate your friendship and leadership. More than that though, I appreciate your godly example. God bless you, my friend.

Contents

TELEVISION

BOOKS

Introduction

"Dad, you're not going to believe this," my daughter told me on the phone one day from her college dorm room. "There's evolution in *My Big Fat Greek Wedding*!"

"You're kidding me," I said. She went on to tell me all the details, and as I hung up the phone, it really hit me. Wow — the years of spending time teaching my children how to think critically had actually paid off. More on that specific example in a later chapter.

It all started with my favorite movie of all time, *The Incredible Mr. Limpet*, played by Don Knotts. I loved that movie when I was growing up and was ecstatic when I found it on VHS.

This will be a great movie for our family night, I said to myself as I raced home to share it with my two children (then 15 and 16), and my wife. Well . . . without giving too much away right now, this "family friendly" movie turns out to be not quite that.

As I look back over the years, I wonder: Why hadn't I caught any of this when I was a child? Well, you see, growing up in the public schools and a liberal church, I had been taught that evolution and the Bible could be combined. You could say I had been desensitized to this kind of content.

But all this changed once my "radar" had been turned on. (I like to use a lot of analogies from my 24-plus years as an air traffic controller at the Chicago O'Hare airport.)

You could say I had a radar system then, but it wasn't plugged in until the 1980s when a pilot challenged me to read Ken Ham's book, *The Lie: Evolution*. It transformed my faith. It caused me to see that I could trust in the truth of God's Word from the very first verse. With God as the master controller and the Bible as the radar, my life was finally set on the right course.

As a Christian who trusted God's Word completely, my radar was now tuned into things of the world that might undermine a Christian's ability to trust the Word of God. My radar became even stronger when I started working for Answers in Genesis and came to a full realization of how evolution and the idea of "millions of years" were used to undermine God's Word. I now picked up the deceptive lies of evolution in places I had never previously thought to look: in television, movies, cartoons, and advertising.

Once I became a Christian, I wanted to teach my children biblical principles such as how to "be in the world but not of the world." Instead of running and hiding from things in the culture, my wife and I chose to teach our children how to think critically. One way we put this into practice was while watching movies. It became a contest to see who could be the first to spot evolution, "millions of years," and other teachings that go contrary to the Word of God. After a while, we had to switch the rules around when we found ourselves starting and stopping the movie so many times. It sometimes took forever to get through a single movie. We decided at that point to just take notes throughout the movie and discuss the movie once it was over.

This regular practice with my children became the inspiration for presentations I now give to churches and youth groups around the country. I ask audience members the following questions: "Do you know we have *400,000 churches and 6,000 first-run theaters* in our country? Now which one do you think impacts our country more?"

Sadly, the answer is always the same — it's theaters. And it's not just about entertainment, I tell the audience. "Hollywood would not spend millions of dollars to *not* try to indoctrinate you," I tell them. Their goal is to get you to think like the world, and their tactics can be subtle. Present the evolutionary content as something "funsy" and cutesy, and suddenly their ideas seem more palatable — that is, if we don't use the Bible as our radar system to keep us from going down the wrong path. Proverbs 3:5–7 tells us that we are to trust in the Lord and not on our own understanding.

In this book, I want you as parents (and kids!) to see three things:

- Some of the powers-that-be in the entertainment industry do have an agenda that is humanistic and anti-Christian.

- Some powers-that-be *do not* have a particular social agenda — they just want to make money off you. We don't want to see a devil behind every bush, as they say.

- Discerning between the two can help you to maintain a healthy family as well as make you more effective in sharing the gospel with a lost culture.

My own research into this topic has yielded some fascinating stuff — showing us average viewers that an evolutionary mindset can reach into every area of the entertainment world. For example, surely no one believes that Michael Crichton's evolutionary world view had no effect on his blockbuster book, *Jurassic Park*. Of course not. Crichton is probably a nice guy; he's obviously talented. But looking at his novels (that have been turned into box-office successes), one can see that his view of origins is totally opposed to the Bible's account of origins.

Here are just a few examples from the world of entertainment:

- Did you know that evolution can be found in classic TV Land shows like *The Munsters?*

- Look at *SpongeBob Squarepants,* and you'll find evolution under the sea.

- Evolution can even be found in many popular family movies like *Lilo and Stitch, Ice Age, Finding Nemo, and The Incredibles*!

- Then you have movies like *Sword and the Stone* which is actually promoted on the Pagan and Wiccans parenting website as a way for parents to get equipped.

Many times, these shows have almost become the "Christian babysitter." We need to be aware of their content. Think about it — the world uses *Finding Nemo, Lilo and Stitch*, and *The Incredibles* to indoctrinate the culture. What has the Church's response been for too long? Flannel graph!!! Please don't misunderstand me, I'm not against flannel graph, but the reality is this — if we try to use flannel graph to reach a young person raised on *Finding Nemo*, we will fail.

I've seen this many times where young folks think we are "out of touch" when we don't communicate with them in a way they understand. Let's be honest — this next generation seems to be biblically illiterate and movie/TV saturated.

Which brings me back to the "origin" of this book.

So what about the movie *My Big Fat Greek Wedding*? Where's the evolution in that? You'll have to read on to see that. Let me assure you that it is there, and most Christians don't catch it until it is pointed out.

Mark 16:15 tells us that we are to "go into all the world and preach the gospel to every creature." Do you suppose that if Christians spent more time witnessing to our lost world and less time being entertained by it, the world wouldn't be so lost?

Here's the thing: we've got many decades of evolutionary teaching behind us. At the time, it felt like entertainment. It looked the part. Sounded like it. But in fact, we taught our children that if the Bible is not true regarding the origin of man, golden retrievers, tree slugs, and stars . . . how can it be true regarding the purpose of Jesus Christ?

As Christians, we need to reflect the Bible's standards and not Hollywood's perverted version of reality.

THE INCREDIBLE MR. LIMPET

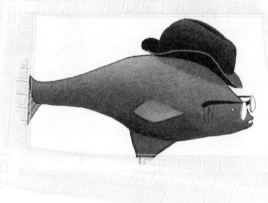

1964

Director
Arthur Lubin

Writers
Jameson Brewer
Joe DiMona (adaptation)

Plot Summary
Milquetoast Henry Limpet experiences his fondest wish and is transformed into a fish.

Actors
Don Knotts, Carole Cook, and Jack Weston

I want to compare two movies and show you just how evolution has covered our culture like an ocean. The first movie, released when I was a kid, really started my whole fascination with evolutionary concepts, because I was watching it one night with my own kids.

The Incredible Mr. Limpet, starring everybody's favorite funnyman, Don Knotts, came along in the years just after a renewed interest in science education in the United States. Our educational culture was shifting from one that at least acknowledged God (through prayer and Bible readings), to one that removed Him altogether. Public policymakers were embracing evolution, prayer was taken out of schools, and television and movies promoting evolution exploded across the country.

As a young person, I loved this movie, so when I saw it in the video store, it was a no-brainer to take it home for family night . . . popcorn, the works! To my surprise, 13 minutes into this family fun event, we had to stop the movie and talk! What in the world could take place that could cause me to stop the movie?

I had forgotten that this engaging movie in the '60s actively promoted an evolutionary concept straight out of the 19th century, in the time of Darwin. Early on, Henry Limpet's wife and best friend are trying to get him out of his apartment. All that ol' Henry wants to do is hang around his apartment, read his book, and watch his fish. His frustrated friend says the equivalent of "What is it with you and these fish?" Henry's response caught me off guard: "Well, I've given it a lot of thought, George, a lot of thought. George, do you realize that our ancestors were fish?"

Whoa! Stop the movie! We gotta talk! I'd never caught this as a young man. I had been raised around the church but never taught how to apply the Bible to the "real" world. I'd never learned to think critically. After discussing this with my children, I turned the movie back on.

Shortly thereafter, Henry's wife and his friend finally get him out of the apartment. They go to Coney Island. On the subway ride there, Henry is still reading his book, oblivious to the world around him. What could be sooo interesting? Hang on!

Once at Coney Island, Henry automatically goes down to the pier to watch the fish. He still has his book under his arm. It's at this point that he (for lack of a better term) "prays." "I wish, I wish, I wish I were a fish!" Keeping in step with Disney, that line in this Warner Brothers movie would not be considered a Judeo Christian "prayer" by any means. But, some deity, whatever it is, heard this "prayer" and the "angels" sing, "Be careful, be careful!" Everything gets dark around Henry, a light then shines on him and he understands something special is about to happen. He smiles and stretches toward the water, eventually falling in.

Henry, who can't swim, then goes through an amazing transformation. Henry Limpet is transformed, stage by stage, from a human into a fish (the reverse of a famous theory by Ernst Haeckel, in which humans allegedly progress from the guppy stage, to fish, to land animals, and finally humans). At one point, at the end of the transformation you see the book that Henry has carried with him up until this time falling behind him in the water. What's this got to do with anything? I've left one piece of information out until now. While standing on the pier, just prior to falling into the water, we see the title of the book. It is entitled *The Theory of Reverse Evolution*. Something interesting occurred to me after watching this as a Christian. Up until this point, everybody was laughing and mocking Henry. Especially, his wife. At one point, his wife tells his friend in a mocking tone as Henry explains evolution, "He's read hundreds of scientific books on the subject. He claims that millions of years ago, there was nothing but fish in the world." Henry: "That's right, and then you see, some of those ancient creatures they became amphibians and they crawled out on land, you see. And then millions of years later they became men!"

Everybody feels sorry for poor, foolish Henry. The movie, though, asserts that HE was right! When he went through the "reverse evolution" process, this was proof positive that Henry was right and that those who don't believe in evolution are wrong.

This movie was entertaining, funny, and was a small part of a cultural shift that embraced evolutionary concepts. Hollywood couldn't have gotten away with that in 1924, or 1944, but you see, attitudes were shifting. The centennial of Darwin's landmark book *On the Origin of Species* had been observed in 1959. The ground had been prepared, so to speak. Or, to think of it another way, the theory of evolution was "in the water," literally.

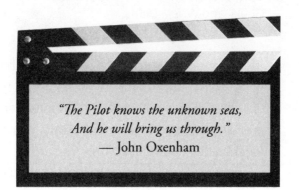

*"The Pilot knows the unknown seas,
And he will bring us through."*
— John Oxenham

FINDING NEMO

**Writer/
Director**
Andrew
Stanton

Plot Summary
Marlin (a clown
fish) is a widower who only has his son Nemo left of
his family after a predator attack. On Nemo's first day
of school, he's captured by a scuba diver and taken
to live in a fish tank in a dentist office. Marlin and his
new absent-minded friend, Dory, set off across the
ocean to find Nemo, while Nemo and his tankmates
scheme on how to get out of the fish tank.

Voices Albert Brooks, Ellen DeGeneres, Alexander
Gould, and Willem Defoe.

Now, flash forward 40 years. The film
animation company Pixar knows children
still love cute fish and underwater color
and an interesting story. So along comes the
blockbuster *Finding Nemo*.

Finding Nemo is great to look at, with plenty
of color and great animation. There are some

good points: a loving father who loves his disobedient son so much he's willing to leave the safety of the reef and go find his lost child (you could even see a parallel between this and Christ coming to save humanity).

There are other things in here that we can use to start conversations.

There's a good one that happens right after Gill has helped Nemo escape from the aquarium back to the ocean. As Gill is put back into the aquarium, all the other fish cheer. Then Gurgle asks Gill a question: "Is he going to be okay, Gill?" Gill's response is interesting, "Don't worry, all drains lead to the ocean!"

This response allows for us to talk about a very serious challenge to the Christian faith today. This challenge is called syncretism. I hear some of you thinking, *What's that?*

Dictionary.com gives us the following definition:

Reconciliation or fusion of differing systems of belief, as in philosophy or religion, especially when success is partial or the result is heterogeneous.

In layman's terms, it works like this: "It doesn't matter what you believe, you just have to believe in something and be sincere." "There are lots of different paths to the top of a mountain. The same is true of religion; all religions lead to God!"

We hear this all the time in our culture today. Recently, singer Willie Nelson expressed this very clearly in an interview he did with *Time* magazine:

I believe that all roads lead to the same place. We're taking different ways to get there, but we all end up in the same place. It's kind of like Kinky Friedman's statement, "May the God of your choice bless you." That's the main thoughts that I have about life (Aug. 7, 2006).

We need to be aware of this belief system and share with Christians that this just isn't the case. According to the Word of God, there is only one way to heaven! At the name of Jesus every knee will bow and tongue confess that Jesus is Lord (Phil. 2:10–11).

Please don't misunderstand me here, I'm not saying that this quote in *Nemo* is teaching syncretism. I believe that you can use it, though, to talk about a topic that is very important to Christians today.

I know by now you are asking, "Where was the evolution in *Finding Nemo*?"

Remember the jellyfish scene? "Give it up, old man! You can't fight evolution. I was built for speed." Wow, what a subtle idea: you can't fight evolution!

You see, the point is, all these things collectively — Henry Limpet's views, "all drains lead to the ocean…" — they come at us every day, from all directions. We are influenced by our surroundings. Evolution and other anti-Christian views build up gradually. Like a drop of water falling into a bucket, each of these things aren't noticed. Nobody's going to drown from a drop of water. But a full bucket or a swimming pool is a different story.

My generation was influenced in part by funny, animated movies. My children's generation is being influenced in part by funny, animated movies. The fact that almost every child in America recognizes Ronald McDonald, while the vast majority couldn't tell you half the Ten Commandments, alerts us that something is very wrong. As parents and children, we have to pay attention to things we're taught, and we must learn that everything must be measured in light of God's Word, which is absolute truth.

"Man is heaven's masterpiece."
— Francis Quarles

The World **VS** The Word

"All flesh is not the same flesh, but there is one kind of
flesh of men, another flesh of animals, another of fish,
and another of birds"
(1 Cor. 15:39).

THE DINOSAUR AND THE MISSING LINK

1915
Silent
Black and white
Animated

Have you heard people say that they long for the "good old days"? The problem is, no one can agree just when the good old days were!

In reality, the only time in world history the term would have applied would have been some short period of time in the Garden of Eden. After that, the best we could do in a fallen world is "the get-through-the-day-by-dealing-with-tough-issues day"!

This thought came to me when researching the 1915 film produced by the famous inventor Thomas Alva Edison. Many in our culture today would look back fondly to those days, before America's involvement in bloody world wars, before assassinations, before a lot of bad stuff. Church attendance was higher then than we have today. People in general understood morality. They understood at least right from wrong. We still had prayer in schools, etc.

But I want to show you that in every age, there are bad influences — wrong philosophies that entice people to abandon faith in Christianity.

Such a philosophy was featured in *The Dinosaur and the Missing Link* film. This was produced in the early "silent picture" days, when Charlie Chaplin was becoming famous for his silly, harmless stories set to film. No one then could have imagined how film would become corrupted in the following decades, culminating in recent releases that in reality deserve an NC-17 rating.

Anyway, *Dinosaur* featured an animated gorilla named "Wild Willie." Willie was the forerunner of animation wizard Willis H. O'Brien's masterpiece, *King Kong* (1933). A synopsis of this film comes from an online review:

> *The Dinosaur and the Missing Link* is set in the Stone Age and relates the simple tale of Theophilus Ivoryhead. The

Duke and Stonejaw Steve vie for the attention of Miss Araminta Rockface, who asks them to provide some meat for their dinner. Meanwhile, Theophilus is sent to catch some fish, causing him to encounter Wild Willie, a large gorilla (O'Brien would later credit him as being King Kong's ancestor), the terror of the countryside who is also hunting for his dinner. During a skirmish with a *Brontosaurus,* Wild Willie falls off the dinosaur's back, hits his head on a stone, and is killed. Theophilus Ivoryhead returns to the cave, proudly standing over his catch, to the disbelief of the others.

This film began to introduce Darwin's evolutionary concepts to movie audiences around the country. It's interesting that O'Brien went on to produce other films for Edison, such as *Prehistoric Poultry*, and later adapted Sir Arthur Conan Doyle's *The Lost World*.

No doubt, O'Brien had been influenced by Darwinian evolution, but the man who bankrolled the films also embraced strange ideas about the world in which we live.

Edison was a contemporary of many of the great men of the age, such as Andrew Carnegie, J.P. Morgan, and Henry Ford. Because they embraced the concept of "the survival of the fittest" (a term created by Darwin's friend Herbert Spencer), they built giant companies on the backs of hard-working employees. They felt entitled to use people in order to amass great wealth. Along the way, they also influenced the way people think about the world.

So the next time we think movies like *Jurassic Park* just arrived on the scene, remember that the philosophy behind it is very old and very influential.

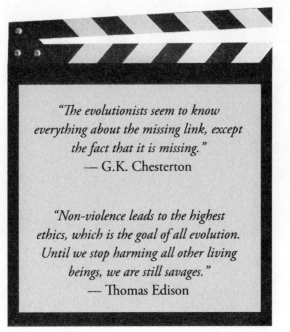

"The evolutionists seem to know everything about the missing link, except the fact that it is missing."
— G.K. Chesterton

"Non-violence leads to the highest ethics, which is the goal of all evolution. Until we stop harming all other living beings, we are still savages."
— Thomas Edison

The World vs The Word

"The LORD God planted a garden eastward in Eden, and there He put the man whom He had formed" (Gen. 2:8).

CREATURE FROM THE BLACK LAGOON

1954

Director
Jack Arnold

Writer
Harry Essex

Actors
Richard Carlson, Julie Adams, Richard Denning

ere's a trivia question that you should get right away if you're paying attention to what page you're on! Which movie opens with these lines: "In the beginning, God created the heavens and the earth, and the earth was without form and void?"

If you guessed something like *War of the Worlds* or *The Day the Earth Stood Still*, you'd be wrong! No, in fact, these lines appear in the cult classic *Creature from the Black Lagoon* — another one of my all-time favorite movies as a young man.

So what's the creature from the Black Lagoon? How does it fit with evolution? In the movie, because its blood composition was halfway between marine life and mammals, it was only able to breathe surface air for a few minutes before it had to return to the water. It also had an outer layer of marine scales that covered a mammalian skin. You see, this was supposedly an evolutionary dead end, one of many transitional forms that didn't survive. This is why it was called the "gill-man," a cross between an amphibian and mammal. Which, by the way, is what we should find if the story of evolution was true. Notice I said "story," because that is exactly what evolution is — a story; science fiction at its finest. At least there is one good use for "evolution" — it makes for great scary movies!

There is an interesting statement made about "bridges" in the movie. After Dr. Carl Maia finds a fossil hand in Devonian-age stone he attempts to assemble a team to go and find the rest of the creature. As they study the bones, Dr. David Reed makes the following statement: "Look, look over here. This lung fish, the bridge between fish and the land animals. How many thousands of ways nature tried to get life out of the sea and onto the land. This one failed; he hasn't changed in millions of years."

I believe that science fiction is very interesting, because when you look at almost all of the classics like *War of* the Worlds, The Thing, etc., it's the same concept. God created this little bacteria millennia ago and that's what killed off the animals. God used and directed evolution or, as a minimum, started the process and let it take its path.

So what's the creature from the Black Lagoon? How does it fit into evolution? "It's a . . . it's a . . . it's a transitional fossil; it's this gill man; he's amphibian but he's human. It's a mixture of these two things; he can breathe air for only a little bit, but then he has to get back into the water so he can breathe on the surface." Do you know what they're trying to tell you? That there is a time-line of 30 million years in which supposedly everything evolved — very rapid evolution — then for 150 million years, nothing changed.

That's what they're talking about with the creature from the Black Lagoon. It evolved, but then it didn't change for 150 million years. Guys, this has been going on for a long time.

The Creature from the Black Lagoon may be a campy, goofy movie to audiences today, but back in 1954, it helped prepare the way for full-blown belief in evolution from water to land creatures. That's how the culture has been "entertained" to believe in evolution.

The World VS The Word

"Then God said, 'Let the waters abound with an abundance of living creatures' " (Gen. 1:20).

"I really don't know why it is that all of us are so committed to the sea, except I think it's because in addition to the fact that the sea changes, and the light changes, and ships change, it's because we all came from the sea. And it is an interesting biological fact that all of us have, in our veins, the exact same percentage of salt in our blood that exists in the ocean, and therefore, we have salt in our blood, in our sweat, in our tears. We are tied to the ocean. And when we go back to the sea — whether it is to sail or to watch it — we are going back from whence we came."

— President John F. Kennedy, 1962

WAR OF THE WORLDS

2005

Director
Steven Spielberg

Writer
Josh Friedman,
David Koepp

Actors
Tom Cruise,
Dakota Fanning,
Miranda Otto

Speaking of science fiction, it doesn't get much better than H.G. Wells. Written just three years after *The Time Machine*, the classic *War of the Worlds* has got to be one of the most influential stories ever written.

The Orson Welles radio adaptation was performed by the Mercury Theatre On The Air on October 30, 1938. The confusion that ensued as a result of people believing this was a true alien invasion is reported to have caused more than 12,000 newspaper articles to be written.

Some people even have suggested that the broadcast was actually a psychological warfare experiment! Hitler was also supposed to have commented on the phenomenon caused by the broadcast. I don't know about that, but I do know this: evolution is front and center of this story. Without evolution and millions of years, there couldn't be any Martians to come and try and take over the earth. I also know this — the story is still having an impact on our culture today. In 2005 alone, there were three new film adaptations released. Not bad for a book written over 100 years ago!

Steven Speilberg's film, starring Scientologist spokesman Tom Cruise, also promotes evolution. At the very end of the movie, Morgan Freeman tells us what happened to the invaders:

> From the moment the invaders arrived, breathed our air, ate and drank, they were doomed! They were undone, destroyed after all of man's weapons and devices had failed by the tiniest creatures that God in His wisdom put upon this earth. By the toll of a billion deaths, man had earned his immunity, his right to survive among this planet's infinite organisms. And that right is ours against all challengers, for neither does man live nor die in vain.

This is another example of that "bridge" from belief to unbelief I talked about in *Creature From the Black Lagoon*. We see the mixing of evolution, millions of years, and God. As a result, more and more we see Christians sell out the absolutes found in the Word of God for a belief system based on man's wisdom. How unfortunate!

MY BIG FAT GREEK WEDDING

SCENE NUMBER 1

2002

Director
Joel Zwick

Writer
Nia Vardalos

Actors
Nia Vardalos, Michael Constantine, John Corbett

So what about the movie *My Big Fat Greek Wedding*? The 2002 sleeper hit, starring Nia Vardalos and John Corbett, features a young woman who finds her dream guy, who marries not only her, but seemingly her whole family, as well. The film rated high as a comedy.

This movie holds a very special place in my heart. No, not because I like girly love movies. In my mind it's a waste of time to go to a movie where nothing is killed and nothing explodes. I'm joking!! No, this movie is special to me because it confirmed in my mind that my wife and I had done the right thing in training our children.

My daughter called me from college and said, "Dad, you're not going to believe it. There's evolution in *My Big Fat Greek Wedding*!" This was very encouraging to us as parents. We had spent time with our children training them to catch these subtle influences, sometimes wondering if they were having any impact. This was confirmation that not only had our children been listening, even though they may have acted as if they weren't, but they were also learning.

Anyway, where's the evolution? Well, it happens when Toula's (the main character's) family is celebrating Easter and her fiancé tries to say "Happy Easter" in Greek to her dad. Her dad is not impressed and says back to him in Greek, which is shown in subtitles, "When my people were writing philosophy, your people were still swinging from trees." Now that's not very subtle, is it?

It's interesting to note that Toula's father has no use for Ian, the fiancé, and there is an element of racial prejudice evident here. Since the time of Darwin, various cultures (especially in Europe — England and Germany come to mind) have seized on his "survival of the fittest" world view, and have projected themselves as "racially superior" to other peoples.

We'll talk more about the impact of science on racism in the Bugs Bunny section. Yes, my buddy Bugs is in the book as well!

It isn't too much of a stretch to say that Toula's father was arrogant enough to believe in the superiority of his culture, and the saturation of Darwinism in society has contributed to this mindset.

I'M A MONKEY'S UNCLE

1948

Directed by
Jules White

Actors
Larry Fine, Moe Howard, Shemp Howard,
Virginia Hunter, Dee Green

It can't get any safer than the Three Stooges, right? Unfortunately there are quite a few episodes involving evolution with the Stooges. Curly is referred to as the "missing link" in more than one episode.

It's been said that some people think the Three Stooges (Moe Howard, Curly Howard, and Larry Fine) created comedy that was primitive: three dumb guys going from one silly, simple plot to the next.

Maybe so, but "primitive" was a hallmark of at least one of their film shorts. Playing cavemen in *I'm a Monkey's Uncle*, the Stooges find themselves in the Stone Age as they gather food. By the way, here we come to an interesting point.

> "So the LORD God caused a deep sleep to fall on Adam, and he slept; and He took one of his ribs, and closed up the flesh in its place. Then the rib which the LORD God had taken from man He made into a woman, and He brought her to the man" (Gen. 2:21–22).

The World VS The Word

Just as *prehistoric* refers to a non-existent time, there is also a false era known as the Stone Age, Bronze Age, or Iron Age, or . . . you get the picture. Evolutionary presuppositions in archaeology presume that in the misty past, evolving man lived in various ages: stone tools, iron tools, bronze tools. In fact, the presence of the tools uncovered by excavators merely means that people living in different environments used different materials for tools. For example, if I find Native American spear points near my home in Kentucky, does that mean Native Americans living here in the 16th century lived in the Stone Age? Of course not! The evolutionists' Stone Age allegedly occurred many thousands of years ago.

Anyway, in the short film, *I'm a Monkey's Uncle*, the Stooges try to fight off other cavemen who happen on the scene and try to steal their women. What was filmed as a slapstick, goofy movie planted an image in viewer's minds — an image of an era that in fact never existed, but exists as a story meant to reinforce the idea of evolution. And that makes me want to beat my head against a wall. Nyuck, nyuck, nyuck!

PLANET OF THE APES

1968

Director
Franklin J. Schaffner

Writer
Pierre Boulle and Michael Wilson

Actors
Charlton Heston, Roddy McDowell, Kim Hunter

In what I consider to be one of the strangest roles of all time, iconic actor Charlton Heston portrayed astronaut George Taylor, who discovers a horrific secret about civilization.

When Taylor's spaceship crashes on a planet far into the future, he discovers that sophisticated apes dominate their human slaves. Emerging from their damaged ship, three astronauts explore the planet, which seems much like their own.

Let's just say bad things happen to Taylor's fellow astronauts, and he finds himself imprisoned in an ape city. A sympathetic ape befriends him, and eventually Taylor escapes with a human woman, who had also been in captivity. Eventually the astronaut discovers that the planet is in fact . . . earth . . . far into the future! It's been taken over by apes!

I will never forget as a child seeing the apes' twitching noses and very expressive faces. Heston captured the confusion and terror of Taylor. But what really struck me years later was that it seemed the producers wanted to portray humans and apes as having "split off" onto separate branches of the evolutionary tree: apes are suddenly running things, while humans have not developed speech.

Then I came across the video that included a brief introduction that confirmed this suspicion. Let me share with you what Charlton Heston had to say about the movie: "A great many people worked long and hard to answer the question of what a civilization would be like if the evolutionary process had been reversed and apes were the superior species."

The one scene that I found very interesting is where Taylor is on trial in front of the three orangutans and Cornelius (Roddy McDowell) tells them: "Yes, behold this marvel, this living paradox, this missing link in an evolutionary chain." When you look at the orangutans, you will see them with in an interesting position. One has his hands over his ears, the next over his eyes and the last over his mouth. This was intentionally done as a parody of the famous "hear no evil, see no evil, speak no evil" monkeys.

The 2001 remake directed by Tim Burton and starring Mark Wahlberg also contained evolutionary teaching. At one point in the movie Capt. Leo Davidson (Wahlberg), makes the following comment: "Talking monkeys can't exist." This isn't received very well, as one of the "talking apes" jumps on him from behind and holds him down, stating: "Apes! Monkeys are further down the evolutionary ladder. Just above humans."

There has been such a move in the past few years toward sympathy for animals — at the expense of humans — that, in that light, one can see the point of the movie. Think about how some people on the left obsess over the well-being of spotted owls, or whales . . . while having utter contempt for humanity, of which they are a part!

> *"Man, whether he likes it or not, is being forced by his nature to seek some higher authority."*
> — Jose Ortega y Gassett

There are 400,000 churches in the United States, and 6,000 movie theaters. Who is influencing our young people the most?

The World VS The Word

"He has made everything beautiful in its time. He has also set eternity in the hearts of men; yet they cannot fathom what God has done from beginning to end" (Eccles. 3:11; NIV).

ICE AGE

2002

Directors
Chris Wedge and Carlos Saldanha

Writers
Michael J. Wilson and Michael Berg

Voices
Ray Romano, Denis Leary, Jack Black,
John Leguizamo, and Goran Visnjic.

The new animation technology is simply amazing. Studios like Disney and Pixar are creating classics along the lines of early favorites *Bambi* and *Fantasia*.

Into this elite class steps *Ice Age*, a movie with funny characters coping with life in, well, the Ice Age. You remember the Ice Age (not literally, I hope): one of those epics when great sheets of glaciers locked continents in ice.

In this movie, so popular with children, we learn of such an age 20,000 or so years ago, in which three characters — a saber-tooth tiger, a sloth, and a woolly mammoth — find a human baby lost in an accident. Of course, the color, characters, and zany plot are all top quality. But notice this amazing quote from an online review of the movie:

> *Ice Age* is at its most amusing in those scenes in which the characters make prescient jokes about their own place in the evolutionary scheme of things. One particularly clever scene involves the three travelers discovering what looks like an underground museum of natural history encased in ice, replete with ancient creatures caught in naturally occurring, chain-of-life exhibits. Like most animated films set in the past, *Ice Age* derives much of its humor through the use of anachronism. We chuckle to hear these creatures applying modern, scientific knowledge to the pre-scientific era in which they are living.

Wow! A lot going on in those comments! Notice the reviewer refers to "scientific knowledge to the pre-scientific era. . . ." This is precisely how modern scholars depict biblical writers: "primitive" thinkers who had no idea about real scientific inquiry.

I like to challenge folks. As we see Sid the Sloth standing with a supposed succession of more complex creatures leading up to him frozen in ice behind him, I ask, "Do you think the writers were trying to imply evolution here?" Almost everyone will say, "Yes!" Then I ask, "Were they successful?" I get the same response most of the time: "Yes."

Let's think critically for a moment. If evolution were true, should we find the various life forms at their various stages all living at the same time? The response is, no, we shouldn't! We should find the least complex in lower geologic layers, thereafter older, and the more complex life forms in more recent layers. They should not be living at the same time. As a matter of fact, that is why the horse series that almost every one of us grew up seeing in school books and museums is an inaccurate portrayal of evolution. Instead of the nice progression that you see in the books and charts, many of those supposed ancestors lived at the same time, making the story impossible.

How sad that our culture, especially the church culture, accepts so meekly the nonsense of evolutionary science.

I don't think that we have to be totally negative when using film clips. There are two fantastic clips in *Ice Age* that we can use to teach critical thinking and open conversations. First, near the beginning, we see animals migrating. Two large animals that appear to be a precursor to the turtle happen to be having a conversation; it's quite funny.

"So where's Eddie?"

"Ahh, he said something about being on the verge of an evolutionary breakthrough."

"Really."

(In the background we see Eddie jumping off of a cliff and crashing to the earth.)

"Some breakthrough!"

This is a wonderful conversation starter. Why, you ask? Think about what those that believe in evolution teach.

Dinosaurs never truly disappeared; they're still here. They just happen to be birds now. Dinosaurs evolved into the birds. That same point is emphasized in *Jurassic Park*.

In order for this to be true, some pretty dramatic changes had to occur. Probably one of the most dramatic changes would be that of a scale evolving into a feather. We really need to understand how silly this is. My friend, Dr. David Menton, was a professor for over 35 years. During this time, he had access to an electron microscope and took thousands of pictures. After seeing just a few of them, I was amazed. There's an old saying, "The devil is in the details." I totally disagree after seeing Dr. Menton's pictures, for "God is in the details."

The more you magnify God's creation, the more amazing it becomes. The story goes like this: over millions of years of time and random chance processes, a scale got "roughed up" and eventually evolved into a feather. During one of Dr. Menton's talks, he shows pictures that compare a feather with a scale. There is *no* comparison. A scale is a fold in the skin while a feather is a complex structure that grows out of the body like a hair. It has one-way hinges, hooks and eyelets that fit exactly, or it wouldn't work. As a matter of fact, God created the original Velcro. It is found in the feather.

Yet our kids get more indoctrination.

The World VS The Word

"From whose womb comes the ice? And the frost of heaven, who gives it birth? The waters harden like stone, and the surface of the deep is frozen" (Job 38:29–30).

FANTASIA

1940

Directors
James Algar, Samuel Armstrong

Writers
Lee Blair, Elmur Plummer

Narrator
Deems Taylor

The great, the classic *Fantasia*. The film that succeeded because Walt Disney gave his illustrators and other creators the flexibility to interpret scenes and characters. The result is a perennial must-see.

But . . . this film was actually used in the public schools to teach evolution. Why would they use this movie in schools? Well, here's the story they tell. In the fourth section of eight, "The Rite of Spring," evolution is animated as millions of years ago, you had this thing the size of a marble and it exploded within a trillionth of a second to everything that we can see, greater than the known universe.

You can watch as it blackens out (that's time passing), and then this hot molten blob cools down as water settles on it. As time passes, amoebas appear in the water. How did you get an amoeba in water? Don't worry about it, it happened. Then the amoeba gets more complex, the scene blackens out, time passes. This is in *Fantasia*? Yeah! And then, over time, the fish appear and they get stronger and stronger and the fins change into limbs, and the fish climbs out onto the land.

Consider also the narration given just prior to starting the segment: "So Walt Disney and his fellow artists have taken him at his word. They have visualized it as pageant. As the story of the growth of life on earth. It's a coldly accurate reproduction of what science thinks went on during the first few billion years of this planet's existence. So now, imagine yourself out in space. Billions and billions of years ago, looking down on this lonely, tormented little planet. Spinning through an empty sea of nothingness."

Wow, I feel uplifted and special, don't you? Contrast that with what God tells us in His Word: "For God so loved the world that He gave His only begotten Son, that whoever believes in Him should not perish but have everlasting life" (John 3:16). This is why we have value — what our loving Creator did for us while we were yet sinners.

You see, this goes all the way back to 1940. Evolution has been indoctrinating through film, and destroying our self-worth at the same time, for a long time.

All this introduces a sort of mysticism (a trait of Disney films), New Age thought, and fantasy. In fact, Disney's Magic Kingdom (which immortalizes *Fantasia* and all the rest of the Disney films in expensive kitsch) sees millions of visitors of all ages every year. There they stand and see a sort of substitute religion, where "if you wish upon a star" all your dreams will come true. Films like *Fantasia*, with silly characters like Mickey Mouse, subtly allow children (and adults!) to substitute the safety and truth of God's Word for magic, fantasy, and unchecked imagination.

*"Before God created the universe,
he already had you in mind."*
— Erwin Lutzer

*"We must wait for God, long, meekly, in
the wind and wet, in the thunder and
lightning, in the cold and the dark. Wait,
and He will come. He never comes to
those who do not wait. He does not go
their road. When He comes, go with Him,
but go slowly, fall a little behind; when
He quickens His pace, be sure of it before
you quicken yours. But when He slackens,
slacken at once; and do not be slow only,
but silent, very silent, for He is God."*
— Frederick William Faber

The World VS The Word

"In the beginning God created
the heavens and the earth"
(Gen. 1:1).

LILO AND STITCH

2002

Directors
Dean DeBlois,
Chris Sanders

Writers
Christ Sanders,
Dean DeBlois

Voices
Daveigh Chase, Chris Sanders,
Tia Carrere, David Ogden Stiers

From an online summary:

In a place far away, illegal genetic experiment #626 is detected: Ruthless scientist Dr. Jumba Jookiba has created a strong, intelligent, nearly indestructible and aggressive being with only one known weakness: The high density of his body makes it impossible for the experiment to swim in water. The scientist is sentenced to jail by the Grand Council of the Galactic Federation. The experiment is to be transported to a prison asteroid, yet manages to escape. With a stolen police cruiser, the destructive being races toward a little and already doomed planet: earth. Stranded on Hawaii, experiment #626 can't actually do much harm. . . . But Dr. Jookiba and the earth expert Pleakley never could have guessed that earth girl Lilo adopts the experiment as a dog, gives him the name Stitch and actually causes an emotional development in the little beast. Her dysfunctional family, consisting only of Lilo and her sister Nani, is about to be ripped apart by social worker Cobra Bubbles. Stitch as the new family member brings action into all their lives and, after a while, not even Pleakley and Dr. Jookiba can recognize their former target. But how shall they bring the news of failure to the Grand Councilwoman without being punished?

Lilo and Stitch is considered a Disney classic already, and words like "heartwarming" are used to describe it. But remember the bridge I mentioned in *Creature from the Black Lagoon*? *Lilo and Stitch* is another segment of that bridge, placing the idea of extraterrestrials in young people's minds. Of course, everyone understands that the character of Stitch is fictional, but the concept of ET life, along with the evolutionary theme of life beginning anew across several epochs combine to make this movie anything but family friendly.

Where is the message of evolution shown in *Lilo and Stitch*? It occurs when Pleakley is telling the Grand Councilwoman that she cannot destroy earth because it is a protected planet. She asks if there is intelligent life on earth, and Pleakley responds with "No," but, it is inhabited by "primitive humanoid life forms" and "every time an asteroid strikes their planet, they have to begin life all over." As Pleakley states this, the Grand Councilwoman sees the picture of an amoeba in the ocean, a fish, a lizard, and so on until you reach man! Not very subtle, but most parents don't catch it.

THE INCREDIBLES

2004

Writer/Director
Brad Bird

Voices
Craig T. Nelson, Holly Hunter,
Samuel L. Jackson

I went to see *The Incredibles*. I know a lot of Christians saw it, because I've talked to them. But . . . who caught the evolution? (And it's not just the fact that they have all the mutations, okay? Yeah, that's part of it.)

Now the premise itself is hilarious:

Mr. Incredible is a superhero; or he used to be, until a surge of lawsuits against superheroes submitted by the people they've saved forced the government to hide them in witness protection programs so they could lead normal, anonymous lives. Now known exclusively by his secret identity, Bob Parr, he lives with his wife Helen, formerly Elastigirl, and their three children, Violet, Dash, and Jack Jack. He works as an insurance claims specialist, and he's fed up with his pushy boss and his immoral profession, but his wife's worked too hard to build a normal life for her family to abide his nostalgia for heroism. When Mr. Incredible is offered the chance to play the role of hero again by a mysterious informant, he jumps at the opportunity, but when it turns out to be a trap set by an old nemesis, the whole family must reveal themselves to save Mr. Incredible and countless innocents.

In fact, the sight of Mr. Incredible running, in his tight superhero outfit and oversized torso on smaller legs, is really very funny.

This one's so subtle! It showed a headline that read, "Scientists Find the Missing Link." My son and I caught it at exactly the same time. But you have to focus on the almost-subliminal message being put into these films. "Missing links" have been deceiving people for 150 years, to the point that millions of people are confused about their origins. The Bible, though, tells us very clearly where we came from, why we're here, and where we're going.

Don't let dazzling cartoons and humorous characters indoctrinate your children.

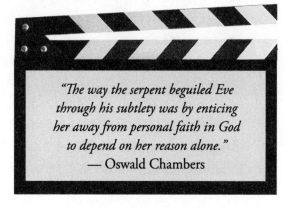

"The way the serpent beguiled Eve through his subtlety was by enticing her away from personal faith in God to depend on her reason alone."
— Oswald Chambers

THE FANTASTIC FOUR

2005

Director
Tim Story

Writers
Mark Frost and Michael France

Actors
Ioan Gruffudd, Jessica Alba, Chris Evans, Michael Chiklis

I grew up in the era of superhero movies and comic books. I was the kid with my eyes glued to a comic book page and, believe me, I'd get lost in it. There's something compelling about superheroes: they can get us out of tight problems, they're generally good, etc. Those qualities make them easy for producers and writers and directors to slip unhealthy world views to unsuspecting audiences. Consider a popular, recent film: *The Fantastic Four.*

In the comic book, which first appeared the year I was born, 1961, Reed, Sue, Ben, and Johnny made up one of the most exciting crime fighting teams that I ever saw. Due to exposure to cosmic rays, Reed could stretch to amazing proportions as if he were made of rubber, Sue could become invisible at will,

Johnny could turn his body into fire, and then there was Ben! Well, Ben became very strong physically, but his body became very ugly and made of "rock." Yet on the inside he hurt from the comments that people made about his appearance. I had a real connection with Ben, better known as the "Thing." I was very overweight as a young man and identified with the pain he felt.

Anyway, where was the evolution in the movie? Reed, while trying to obtain funding from his future archenemy, Victor von Doom, tells him, "My research suggests that exposure to a high-energy cosmic storm-fallen solar wind might have triggered the evolution of early planetary life."

There are other issues in this movie, though, that I think we need to point out. It is important to recognize the messages that are being given throughout the movie.

In the movie, why did Sue leave Reed? To be frank, this shocked me. Even though I know it shouldn't, it still caught me off guard. Sue and Reed are in a heated discussion over why they broke up:

Sue: "I was ready for the next step, you weren't. Ergo, I walked."

Reed: "I think it's a little more complicated than that."

Sue: "I just wanted to share an apartment."

What??? The next step in a relationship is to "share an apartment"? Whatever happened to the days of "First comes love, then comes marriage, then comes Carl with a baby carriage"? Do you see the morality that's being taught in the movies?

Be careful, friends, be very careful. We need to show that this is NOT the normal progression of a relationship. This is a sin-distorted depiction of a wonderful relationship that God wants us to enjoy. The rightful place for sex is inside the bonds of a loving marriage, based on the Word of God, with a follower of Jesus Christ. The day of "missionary" dating and marriages must come to an end. Parent, young person, we have to quit allowing our feelings and wisdom to dictate what is proper in our relationships. God tells us that there is a way that seems right to man — in the end though, it leads to death. To see women so cavalier about living with men prior to marriage really bothered me.

Single person, you need to know the truth about marriage. Ephesians 5:21–33 gives us the "blueprint" for a proper marriage. Trust God, not man, on this, and you will be much happier in life.

There's another interesting point in the movie that we should point out as well. As Ben is trying to have a drink, he breaks the glass because he is so strong and can't control it. He looks up to heaven and says, "If there's a God, He hates me." His future girlfriend, a blind lady, responds with, "She . . . is not so into hate." What's being taught here? I cannot state with 100 percent certainty, but, I can say that what she is saying is consistent with the Wiccan religion. If you think that I'm a little paranoid here, I don't blame you. If you do a search on the Internet, though, you will find a website dedicated to Pagan and Wiccan parents. On this site they give ideas on how to raise your children to have open minds. One of their suggestions is to watch Disney's *Sword in the Stone*. Interesting! Even the secular world knows that movies impact children's thinking.

Christian, we need to wake up.

The World VS The word

"And I, because of their actions and their imaginations, am about to come and gather all nations and tongues, and they will come and see my glory"
(Isa. 66:18; NIV).

SPIDER-MAN

2001

Director
Sam Raimi

Writer
David Koepp

Actors
Tobey Maguire, Willem Dafoe, Kirsten Dunst

I've already told you that I was a comic book geek as a kid. Spider-Man was my all-time favorite as a young man.

I love to mess around with students when I get a chance. I'll ask the question, "Why does Spider-Man have his powers?" Almost always, I get the response, "Because he got bit by a spider!" Then I ask, "What kind of spider?" The response normally is, "A radioactive spider!" Ahh, now I understand. That is the "old school" explanation. You middle-aged folks, like myself, will remember the song: "Spider-Man, Spider-Man, does whatever a spider can. Is he strong? Listen, bub, he's got radioactive blood. Hey there, here comes the Spider-Man."

Why would they change the spider and lose an all-time classic tune like that? That's what they did, though! In the movie, what kind of a spider was it? It was a "genetically engineered spider."

The reason they did this is because scientists now know that radiation does not produce beneficial mutation, it destroys. For instance, there is no hope to get a scale to evolve into a feather by using radiation. The only possible way that you could get new information in the genome is by genetically enhancing or altering the animal. *Not* radiation. So where's the evolution in Spider-Man? Consider that when Willem Dafoe's character, Norman Osborn, is about to take a serum, which eventually changes him into the Green Goblin, he justifies it by stating, "Forty thousand years of evolution and we've barely even tapped the vastness of human potential."

As a young man, one thing that I really would liked to have had was *spider sense*; I mean, spider sense was like the best thing going. You knew when something was coming. Your senses were heightened. I wish I'd had spider sense as I've grown older. Now that I'm an adult, I realize that I'll never get spider sense. But you know, there's something that's even better than spider sense. It's called *Bible sense*.

God has given us a record: He's the only one who's always been there, He's given us a true history book to be able to deal with the world that we're living in. You can have Bible sense when you start from the Word of God to understand the world that we live in, to have answers to real issues. Why don't we do it? We've been trained to put on those glasses to think like the world. The average time a child in America spends in school each year is 900 hours, the average time a child in America spends in front of the television set is 1,023 hours. Christian, how many hours do we spend in school versus how many hours do we spend in church? Oh, we go to church every week. We still have Sunday evening services. Wow! Two hours a week? We still have a Wednesday evening service. Three hours a week.

Do you think in 3 hours a week you're going to over-come over 1,900 hours of very focused indoctrination? Then you go to the church and you get the schizophrenic message "You can't trust the Bible about creation, but Jesus loves you and has a wonderful plan for your life." It's true that Jesus has a special plan for your life, but we have to stop thinking like the world! I'm passionate about this! Talk about climbing the walls when I hear Christians disconnect their faith from the real world!

Spider-Man had some advantages, but you'll never have the complete package until you realize there's only one true Superhero, and He's been here since before the beginning of the world. He has all the answers for your life.

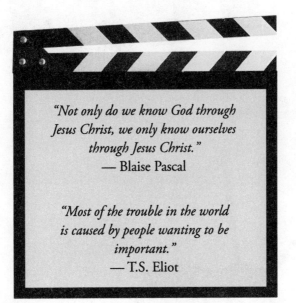

"Not only do we know God through Jesus Christ, we only know ourselves through Jesus Christ."
— Blaise Pascal

"Most of the trouble in the world is caused by people wanting to be important."
— T.S. Eliot

The World **VS** The Word

"But he was wounded for our transgressions" (Isa. 53:5).

CSI

CBS TV series
2000–Present

Creator
Anthony Zuiker

Head staff writer
Anthony Zuiker

Actors
William Peterson, Marg Helenberger,
David Caruso, Gary Sinese

One of the latest franchise television series is set in Las Vegas. No, wait, New York. Wait a minute, I mean, Miami.

Actually, CSI is three shows, all set in those exotic locales. All are slickly produced by film and TV producer Jerry Bruckheimer, who combines compelling story lines with cool clothes and sets. "CSI Las Vegas" was the first, propelling William Peterson's "Gil" to fame. The show was such a hit that it spawned (there's a cool word) two others.

The premise is that a team of forensic scientists, besides their field work, solve murder cases and occasionally are involved in shootouts. It's riveting TV.

> "Therefore God also gave them up to uncleanness, in the lusts of their hearts, to dishonor their bodies among themselves" (Rom. 1:24).

The World VS The Word

Isn't it interesting that even in a fairly mild show like this . . . evolution creeps in? Do we really think there aren't world view messages inserted in shows like this? In one episode, Gil Grissom is discussing the sexuality of a person: "There are two male oysters, and one of them can change genders at will, and before man crawled out of the muck, maybe he had the same option. Maybe originally we were supposed to be able to switch genders and being born with just one sex is a mutation."

No messages there, right? I mean that's just police detective stuff, right? Guys — these messages are there! Shows like this aren't just about great camera angles and cliff-hanger plots. They also indoctrinate people in unbiblical ideas — in the above case by making homosexuality a random evolutionary happening.

BOB THE BUILDER

PBS Kids series
1999–Present

Creator
Keith Chapman

Voices
Neil Morrissey, Kate Harbour

What can possibly be wrong with a colorful little construction character like Bob? He's cutesy, colorful, friendly. Besides, anybody with friends like Muck, Scoop, and Lofty has to be a nice guy, right?

In fact, Bob has become such a hit that there's a whole line of products that has stamped his image indelibly in young minds. Such a character can be used for great good or great harm. In this case, a simple character and his simple settings are used to push the millions-of-years line, still one of the biggest stumbling blocks to the gospel for people all over the world. Again, they're starting with young children. "Bob the Builder" is specifically designed to appeal to children between the ages of two and five.

"Bob the Builder" has a major potential to influence our children's world view. Unfortunately, many times it is not a view their parents would approve of. People might laugh at me for going to this "safe stuff," but . . . well, just consider for yourself.

You know, they actually produced a show entitled "Scoops the Stegosaurus":

> Bob: "Hold it, Scoop! There's something down there! It's too big to be a cow's bone, but it just might be . . . a dinosaur's bone!"
>
> Lofty: "A, a, a, a, dinosaur!"
>
> Bob: "It's all right, Lofty, the dinosaurs lived millions of years ago."

Friends, these messages are there, over and over and over again.

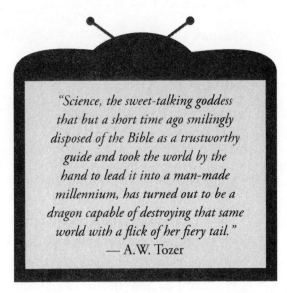

"Science, the sweet-talking goddess that but a short time ago smilingly disposed of the Bible as a trustworthy guide and took the world by the hand to lead it into a man-made millennium, has turned out to be a dragon capable of destroying that same world with a flick of her fiery tail."
— A.W. Tozer

FRIENDS

NBC TV series 1994–2004

Creators
David Crane, Marta Kauffman

Actors
Jennifer Anniston, Courtney Cox, Lisa Kudrow, Matt LeBlanc, Matthew Perry, David Schwimmer

You know, I'm sometimes surprised at how aggressive certain shows are in promoting evolution, and the byproducts of that type of thinking: casual sex, lying, homosexuality. One such show was NBC's "Friends," a zany group of 20-somethings who spent a decade stumbling through life. I've talked to more than one person who thought the first season was funny, but then noticed a cynical streak. I've seen maybe one episode, but my daughter called me after viewing one in which Mr. Darwin was discussed.

The episode, "The One Where Heckles Dies" (1995, episode 3) portrayed a doubter of evolution as an imbecile. The dialogue went something like this:

> Phoebe: "I don't know, it's just, you know, monkeys, Darwin you know — it's a, it's a nice story, I just think it's a little too easy."
>
> Ross: "Too easy, too, the process of every living thing on this planet evolving over millions of years from single-celled organisms is, is too easy?"
>
> Phoebe: "Yeah, I just don't buy it!"
>
> Ross: "Uh excuse me; evolution is not for you to buy, Phoebe; evolution is scientific fact like, like, like the air we breathe! Like gravity!"

Notice, too, that the character of Phoebe, who in this episode is questioning evolution, is the "ditzy" character on the show — the dumb blonde who's often confused.

Also, notice the argument that Ross uses to show Phoebe is wrong. *Evolution is scientific fact. . . . Like gravity.* If parents teach their children some basic answers, they would be able to answer this type of false claim (which, by the way, is used by evolutionists quite often). First, we need to teach our children how to tell the difference between "observational science" and "historical science."

Observational science involves making "observations," in the present, then using our five senses to conduct experiments to see if what we believe is true. This would

> "If anyone teaches false doctrines and does not agree to the sound instruction of our Lord Jesus Christ and to godly teaching, he is conceited and understands nothing"
> (1 Tim. 6:3; NIV).

The World (VS) The Word

include fields of study such as astronomy, biology, geology, etc. Creationists and evolutionists all have the same "observational science." We all have the same fossils, people groups, stars, etc. The problem isn't in the "evidence," it is in the interpretation of evidence.

Historical science is where the problems start to occur. This entails what we *believe* about the past. The problem with this is that our "beliefs" about the past cannot be observed, and that our world view will greatly affect the way that we understand the evidence.

Can we use observational science to test gravity? Absolutely! Pick up anything and then drop it. Hmm! Interesting — gravity works. Do it again. Hmm! Amazing — it still works.

Now let's do the same thing with "evolution." Using observational science, how do we test it? There is no test. Equating "gravity" with "evolution" is NOT the same thing.

After watching *Friends*, all we've ended up with is a culture confused about origins and morality. And that's not funny at all.

Geico Insurance

In 2004, the Geico Company began a series of TV advertisements that have achieved gold status: they are discussed and laughed about all over the country (the goal of good advertising!).

Many feature a cute (Australian) gecko, but a couple of others are helping perpetuate the myth that early man evolved from hominids into Neanderthals.

In one, a company executive is wining and dining two men in an upscale restaurant. He has already offended them by assuming they are less intelligent because they have the classic Neanderthal features: thick forehead and brows, protruding jaw, and tangled hair. It's the kind of image you've seen in textbooks for 40 years.

In an interesting twist, the two "Neanderthals" turn out to be quite intelligent, with precise grammar and high vocabulary skills. When the executive urges them to order lunch, they both glare at him. One orders a fancy dish, while the other claims to no longer have an appetite.

It's funny stuff, until you realize the premise behind it is that we have evolved from ancient, transitional creatures who clubbed their women and lived savage lives.

Ironically, at Answers in Genesis we believe early man *was* incredibly intelligent. In fact, the alleged evolving creatures known as Neanderthals would have been at least as intelligent as we are today. They were simply people who lived in hostile environments — an Ice Age brought on by the great flood of Noah's time.

BUGS BUNNY

Warner Brothers
1938–Present

Creators
Chuck Jones, Friz Freleng,
Tex Avery

Voices
Mel Blanc

Folks, this one hurts. I grew up with Bugs, just as millions of others did. Wikipedia refers to him as "a fictional, street-smart grey rabbit."Bugs tormented, teased, and bumfoozled (is that a word?) a succession of hilarious characters such as Elmer Fudd, Yosemite Sam, and Daffy Duck. The wise-cracking Brooklyn/Bronx Bugs has become an icon in celluloid. So what's my beef with this hare?

One short is titled "Pre-hysterical Hare." It starts off with Bugs running (because he's being chased by Elmer, of course!). He jumps over a hedge and the land gives way as he falls into a "prehistoric" cave. Now did you catch that wording? "Prehistoric." Christian, think biblically — is there any such thing as "prehistoric"? Not in the Bible, there isn't. "Prehistoric" is a man-made evolutionary term that suggests a very ancient past, long before man. Genesis 1 is the beginning of *time*, the beginning of *history*, so there is no such thing as prehistoric. This one tiny word shows how man's "wisdom" — evolution/millions of years — has infiltrated our way of thinking and that we've been taught to think like the world.

Anyway, inside the cave, Bugs finds a time capsule; inside the time capsule he finds a film, so he takes the film and puts it on at home. Bugs: "There, it's all set up." The film intro is clever: "A MICRONESIAN FILM DOCUMEN-TARY in CROMAGNONSCOPE COLOR BY NEANDERTHAL COLOR" and on they go. Did you catch all the allusions to evolution in there?

What's the short about? Well, it's about life *a long time ago* — everything was hunting and killing and only the best hunters survived. Who was the best hunter? Elmer Fuddstone. What did he hunt? Why, the saber-toothed wabbit, of course!

Narrator: "Yes, the saber-toothed rabbit, his natural habitat is deep in the lush jungle."

Bugs: "Oh, brudder, get a load of that snaggletooth aboriginally heh, heh, heh, heh. . . ." "Hey now, there's something mighty familiar-looking

75

about that joker. Could it be that he's one of my ancestors?"

Snaggletooth: "Nyah, could be!"

Right about now, your biblical radar should be going off!

I had one reporter mock me on this point. Jason Cohen, in an article entitled "In Genesis They Trust," published in *Cincinnati Magazine,* said, "You want to say: Chill out, dude. Bugs Bunny's a cartoon! Fiction. Art. Narrative. Allegory. Don't take things so, errrr . . . *literally.*"

I disagree. The Aborigines of Australia, because of evolutionary thinking and the teaching of "millions of years," were thought for a long time to be the closest living group to prehistoric man. This characterization caused them tremendous misery. There were even manuals printed, teaching how to hunt Aboriginals. They were also skinned and their skins sent to museums in England to be stuffed and put on display. Their heads were cut off and boiled down so scientists could study their skulls.

Ultimately, between five and ten thousand graves were desecrated and their bones sent to museums to be studied and put on display. As a matter of fact, many of their bones are still there and will not be returned to the descendants for a proper burial until laws are changed to allow this to happen.

A newspaper reported that "scientists here are concerned that if these bones go back, their value for scientific research will be lost forever" (*USA,* 10/08/03, by Nicholas Glass).

How sad! Scientists are more concerned about keeping the bones rather than allowing their descendants to have a proper burial.

How could this happen? Consider this: the original title of Charles Darwin's now-famous book is *On the Origin of Species by Means of Natural Selection; or, the Preservation of Favoured Races in the Struggle for Life*.

If this is the case, some "races" are closer to the "missing link" than others, so what is wrong with wiping out "inferior" species? We don't breed inferior cattle — why let inferior people breed? If you can dehumanize something, it is very easy to get away with things that are unbelievable.

Ultimately, only because the Bible is true can we say this is wrong. Yes, Christians have made mistakes in the past and allowed racism and racist thoughts to influence them as well as the church. The major difference is that we were "inconsistent" with the Bible when we did this. Friends, do you realize that this behavior is completely consistent with an evolutionary world view though?

Sorry, Jason, I don't find that very funny, personally, and taught my children to not accept that sort of thinking from any source, cartoon or otherwise.

The World VS The Word

"So then, each of us will give an account of himself to God" (Rom. 14:12).

In the big scheme of things, it's not good to talk about different human "races" and ancient hominids, because there is only one race, the human race. Ironically, at the time Bugs Bunny emerged, horrific racial ideas were the norm. Because of people's belief that Aboriginals were the closest living relatives to the missing link, all kinds of ugly things happened.

Not only did these things happen in Australia, they happened here in the United States. Up until 1967, 16 states had laws on the books making it unlawful for a person with one drop of "non-white" blood to marry a white person. Over 60,000 people were coercively sterilized in the United States because they were "white trash," the wrong race, or "feeble minded." Dallas Theological Seminary wouldn't accept a black person from America into their institution as a student until 1969. As a matter of fact, Hitler's "scientists" took all the research done by "scientists" here in America and ultimately implemented it in Germany. This led to the outright murder of millions of human beings.

What really bothers me about all this is that during the 1940s, '50s, and early '60s, most people would admit that America was, at least on the surface, more Christian than today. I mean, teachers could talk about God openly or even pray. Displays of the Ten Commandments weren't a problem and you could even say "Merry Christmas" in public and not be embarrassed! How could this "Christian" nation pass anti-Christian laws? I ask those who attend my speaking events, "Which were we consistent with when we passed those laws, man's opinion or God's Word?" There is no question, we allowed man's opinion to be raised to a higher standard than God's Word and we passed laws consistent with our world view. And to be frank, we blew it! Friends, we have to be very careful with what we allow to be the foundation of our thinking. I've talked about messages like this with my family, and I think you should, too. Sorry, Bugs.

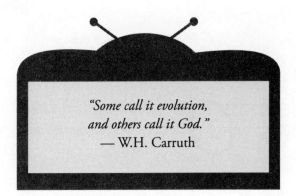

"*Some call it evolution,
and others call it God.*"
— W.H. Carruth

The World VS The word

"By pride comes nothing but strife, but with the
well-advised is wisdom"
(Prov. 13:10).

SPONGEBOB SQUAREPANTS

Nickelodeon
1999–Present

Creator
Stephen Hillenburg

Voices
Tom Kenny, Rodger Bumpass,
Bill Fagerbakke, Clancy Brown

*O*hhhhh, who lives in a pineapple under the sea? SpongeBob Squarepants!"

This little refrain is every bit as popular as the "Howdy Doody" theme was in another era. In fact, I'd say that the little yellow sea character, SpongeBob Squarepants, is so popular, he'll one day take his place in the Cartoon Hall of Fame (is there one?).

Sure, I'm old, but I just don't get it! A sponge wearing pants, living underwater?!! In at least one episode there's lightning, there's rain, there's fire! Then there's a squirrel running around with some sort of helmet on so it can breathe — it's just dumb! His friend Patrick is so dumb, he manages to be hilarious. (Some around the Answers in Genesis complex accuse me of being the inspiration for Patrick!)

> "Have you entered the springs of the sea? Or have you walked in search of the depths?"
> (Job 38:16).

The World VS The Word

Yet, even here, evolution has clawed its way into our consciousness. One episode, called "Ugh," paid homage to the god of evolution: "Ahhh! Dawn breaks over the primordial sea. It is here that millions of years ago life began taking its first clumsy steps out of the darkness, opening its newly formed eyeballs to stare into the blinding light of intelligence."

So even in *SpongeBob*, there's evolution. People have chastised me for taking issue with cartoon characters like this, but again, I'm simply providing evidence that Darwin is alive and well in the 21st century. His ideas have permeated Western thought for more than a century. The people who have the creativity to fashion memorable cartoon characters are also people who grew up with little or no biblical instruction. And they are passing on what they believe to you and your children.

FedEx

During the Super Bowl, there was one commercial that I really enjoyed. Remember the caveman who tied the stick to the *pterodactyl* and sent it off to deliver the "package"? Immediately, the poor delivery lizard is eaten by *T-rex*!

To make matters worse, the caveman is fired by his "boss" for not using FedEx, even though there is no such thing at that time. I found it very funny, although the message of evolution was very clear. I like to use it in a different way, though. This commercial drives those that believe in evolution and an earth life of millions of years crazy! Why? (Good question, thanks for asking!) Because, according to the evolutionary belief system, men and dinosaurs are separated by millions of years, and there is no way that even cavemen lived at the same time as the dinosaur. For a Bible-believing Christian, though, this isn't a problem! Now, we do have a problem with the picture of a brutish, low-brow hominid that is unable to speak, grunting until language evolves, which is depicted in this commercial. But we have no problem with man and dinosaur living together.

"So far, evolution has been nothing but staggering from one error to the other."
— Henrik Ibsen

JIMMY NEUTRON

Nickelodeon
2001–Present

Based on the 2001 film *Jimmy Neutron: Boy Genius*

Director/Writer
John A. Davis

Voice
Debi Derryberry

Jimmy Neutron . . . sorry to say, this show's full of evolution. Again, the characters in this are so lovable, it seems a shame to bring up unpleasantness, but I suppose the evolution had to creep in, since the film dealt with outer space. Astronomy is a stronghold of evolutionary teaching. Think about it — any time there are aliens involved, evolution has to be present. The only way that we can get "aliens" is for evolution to have taken place. We hear this over and over again from the media. Life evolved a certain way here on earth and would have evolved differently on other planets. Therefore, we get the various life forms that fill the TV and theaters.

The particular episode I'm citing had just a tiny reference, yet it held so many implications.

In "Substitute Creature," Jimmy and his pals find a piece of 64-million-year-old spinach in between some teeth on a dinosaur museum exhibit. They clone it and bring it back to life. Now that's ridiculous, right? Come on, that's just ridiculous — 64-million-year-old spinach! It wouldn't last that long!

Something interesting has been taking place in paleontology circles. Let me share a real story with you on this. Recently we had some reporters from England visit the AiG headquarters. I had the privilege of showing them around. I could tell they were uncomfortable as they filmed parts of the Creation Museum. The one exhibit that really bothered them was where we show humans and dinosaurs co-exisiting. I was friendly and just visited with them the entire time. After about an hour, "Tom" finally felt comfortable enough to really talk "to" me, not "at" me. He waited until his friends weren't around then asked me, "Carl, you can't really believe that dinosaurs and man lived together, can you?"

What a wonderful opportunity! I responded this way: "Tom, let me change your starting point. The problem isn't the evidence, it's how we look at it. Here, let me show you what I mean. We are finding dinosaur bones that are 100 percent bone, not showing any mineralization. As a matter of fact, attached to some of those bones there is tissue, and inside the tissue there are pliable blood vessels, and when they squeezed them, red blood cells came out! Come on, Tom, you really can't believe that this lasted 70 million years, can you?"

And this appears to be exactly what is being found in our world today. Evolutionist as well as creationist fossil hunters have in fact discovered dinosaur bones that appear to not be fossilized in the least! (In fact, AiG's own Buddy Davis was on one of these expeditions to Alaska a few years ago.) In addition, unfossilized bone marrow was recently found inside of frog fossils. Christian, we don't have a problem here. There is absolutely no way that bone marrow, tissue, blood cells, bones, etc. could last 70 million years without totally decaying into nothing.

Yet these evolutionists say, in essence, "Oh there must be some method out there that saves this stuff for millions of years that we just don't know about." How about this for an answer: *It's not 70 million years old!* Tom couldn't answer the question and neither can any other person who believes in evolution or millions of years. Please pray for him; I am.

This tiny insertion of such a ridiculous concept — spinach in a fossil must be 70 million years old — is a tactic used by evolutionists to further their world view. Don't be fooled. If we don't have answers to this or fail to teach our children how to answer the claim, we are missing a very unique opportunity to *use* the culture and not be *abused* by the culture.

"*The world was built in order and the atoms march in tune.*"
— Ralph Waldo Emerson

"*Man is the greatest miracle and the greatest problem on this earth.*"
— David Sarnoff

The World VS The Word

"Have you ever given orders to the morning, or shown the dawn its place . . . ?"
(Job 38:12; NIV).

GILLIGAN'S ISLAND

CBS TV series
1964–67

Creator
Sherwood Schwartz

Actors
Bob Denver, Alan Hale Jr.

When I was growing up, one of the major questions making the rounds was the rather important, "So who's better looking, Ginger or Mary Ann?" This was referring to the two stranded beauties on the quirky "Gilligan's Island." Okay, so maybe the question was only important to teenage boys!

At any rate, the show, about seven people stranded on an uncharted island after a storm during a pleasure cruise, became TV legend. It has been shown continuously in reruns since it went off the air. Bob Denver, as Gilligan, and his sidekick, the Skipper (played by veteran TV actor Alan Hale Jr., son of film star Alan Hale Sr.) engaged in hilarious shenanigans as they tried repeatedly to find their way back to civilization. In fact, the running jokes involving radios made out of coconuts, diet staples like coconut cream pies, and loony characters who surfaced, have all become part of television lore.

It almost goes without saying, but the episodes themselves were so hokey, no one could take them seriously. There was the one about Gilligan having a nightmare and awakening to think he was a vampire. Then there was the one about the castaways eating radioactive vegetables, which gave them super powers (carrots helped them locate ships way out at sea).

But one, "The Secret of Gilligan's Island," (episode 93, aired March 13, 1967) involved the discovery of ancient stone tablets written in "prehistoric hieroglyphics." Catch the use of the word "prehistoric" again. The castaways began to believe the tablets could lead to them getting off the island. Anyway, later on Gilligan has a dream; in the dream, Gilligan and the rest of the castaways are cavemen and women trying to escape the island, and they run into a *T. rex* dinosaur. This, of course, upsets evolutionists again by showing dinosaur and man living at the same time.

During the decade this episode aired, public science curriculum was being slanted heavily toward the evolutionary view. I remember studying, with fascination, artists' renderings of "cavemen" in textbooks.

Do you realize that the Bible actually talks about "cave men"? Check it out for yourself in Hebrews 11:38. Yet the whole concept of "prehistoric" man evolving into present-day man is ludicrous, and ultimately is a serious impediment to the gospel.

89

THE MUNSTERS

CBS TV series
1964–66

Directors
Norman Abbott, David Alexander

Writers
Tom Adair, James B. Allardice

Actors
Fred Gwynne, Yvonne De Carlo,
Al Lewis, Butch Patrick

Loveable monster Herman Munster (played by Fred Gwynne) was actually portrayed as a "missing link" in at least two episodes of this cult-classic show.

In episode 63, "Prehistoric Munster" (see a recurring theme in these shows? Hint: *prehistoric*), Marilyn sculpts a likeness of Herman. When her art professor sees Herman's likeness, and Marilyn tells him it's based on a real person, the professor dreams of making money by "unveiling" a living missing link.

In episode 2 (1965) "Herman, the Master Spy," a Russian fishing trawler picks up a scuba-diving Herman in its haul of fish and mistakes him for the missing link.

We can't, of course, think that every insertion of evolutionary dogma was the result of a conspiracy. Certainly, evolution had been making inroads into public schools for years, although the prehistoric/missing link/caveman stock character in the '60s was, by and large, meant as comedy. Still, it's sad to see funny shows like "The Munsters" used to place evolutionary images in viewers' minds.

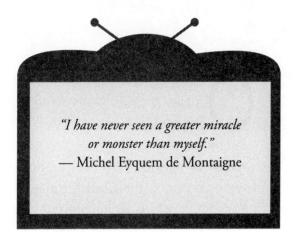

"I have never seen a greater miracle or monster than myself."
— Michel Eyquem de Montaigne

LAW
& ORDER

NBC TV series
1990–present

Creator
Dick Wolf

Actors
Sam Waterston, Jerry Orbach, Michael Moriarity, Jill Hennessey, Benjamin Bratt

One of my favorite shows on television is *Law & Order* — much to my wife's chagrin! It seems like I watch it about five times a day.

I saw an episode that I think embodies what I see going on in the Church today. You see, our children ask us legitimate questions, and we can't answer them. Our response is either a joke or an annoyed non-answer. I've see this many times: a child will ask about dinosaurs, or where did all the water go from Noah's flood. Because the parents don't know themselves — they've been confused by the evolutionary erosion in confidence in God's word — no one has a satisfying answer. The *Law & Order: Special Victims Unit* episode I refer to was titled "Control," and illustrates this. Notice this dialogue:

> Granddaughter: "Grandpa, who made the world?"
> Grandfather: "That's a tough one, Sunshine"
> Granddaughter: "Why?"
> Grandfather: "Well, because some folks say God made it, and others say there was this big bang and the world just appeared."
> Granddaughter: "I don't think so."
> Grandfather: "Who do you think made the world?"
> Granddaughter: "Bob the Builder, that's his job."

People laugh when I play a clip of this episode in front of audiences, and on one level, it is funny. But we've got to remember that we can have confidence in God's Word. We can tell our children that Genesis tells us exactly how the world came to be. I challenge those in attendance, "Are you ready to answer that question?" You see, we have to be ready to answer that question. God commanded us to be prepared to give an _____ (you fill in the blank) for the reason for the hope that lies within us.

A. opinion
B. suggestion
C. answer/defense
D. I don't know!

JURASSIC PARK

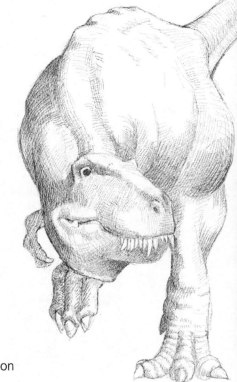

Author
Michael Crichton

C richton, the fabulously successful author and doctor, has a dilemma: practice medicine or write best-selling novels? Tough problem to have!

Anyway, Michael Crichton wrote *Jurassic Park* years ago, and Steven Spielberg directed the film, based on the book. For pure entertainment, you would be hard-pressed to top it. Grand island scenery, clever plot, and most of all, those "terrible lizards . . . bigger than life!"

The premise centers on "dino DNA" used to produce a whole community of various dinosaurs on a remote island. You can guess what happens; the same thing that happens every time man tries to tame nature.

Needless to say, most people see the plot of this book as pure entertainment, although some serious people have speculated that we could reintroduce dinosaurs to our world. I doubt it, but Crichton has brought about some destructive qualities from the message of the book, which is heavily evolutionary. As Dr. Ray Bohlin has pointed out in his essay on the subject, the "owl-like hoots" of the dilophosaur are purely made up; no one can know what a dinosaur sounded like. But this alleged, shared trait of dinosaurs and birds "proves" they are linked genetically.

What is so important about the DNA? Well, without it there could be no Jurassic Park. Here's how it works. Scientist finds a mosquito inside of supposedly millions-of-years-old amber. Fortunately for scientists, this mosquito sucked the blood of a dinosaur prior to landing on a tree and getting entrapped in the tree sap which became amber over time.

Millions of years later, scientists find these mosquitoes and extract the dinosaurs DNA from them. Using this DNA, they then bring these extinct creatures back to life.

Our radar should be going off here for a couple of reasons. First, isn't it interesting that they find mosquitoes that they believe are up to 100 million years old and they are exactly the same as the tiny menaces we see today?

Not only did mosquitoes not change after these supposed millions of years of time, but many other things such as birds, fish, bats, plants, etc. also have not changed.

This isn't a problem for Bible-believing Christians. God told us He created a variety of different animals, plants, etc. If this is true, this is what we should find. Amazingly, this is what we do find!

Secondly, how could DNA last millions of years without being destroyed? DNA is self-destructing and it should not be able to last vast amounts of time.

Again, Bible-believing Christians would expect to find DNA because it's not millions of years old.

Crichton's clever use of dialogue and interplay between the characters of his novel presented a foundation of evolution for his readers. Unfortunately, this carried over to the movie, giving a whole new generation of kids a false view of earth history.

It just goes to show you the old saying is true: you can't always believe what you read.

The World VS The Word

"The earth was without form, and void; and darkness was on the face of the deep. and the Spirit of God was hovering over the face of the waters" (Gen. 1:2).

> *"A house testifies that there was a builder, a dress that there was a weaver, a door that there was a carpenter; so our world by its existence proclaims its Creator, God."*
> — Rabbi Akiba Ben Joseph

> *"The universe is centered on neither the earth nor the sun. It is centered on God."*
> — Alfred Noyes

NeanderThin

Author
Ray Audette with Troy Gilchrist

I recently saw a television program that claimed the change in public school students' diets in the '60s and '70s contributed greatly to increased weight gain that we can see all around us today. I learned that if we'd go back to the way we ate before that, obesity might disappear. Maybe so, but get a load of the following "health tip"!

Description:

Discover the diet that's been working for thousands of years! In a revolutionary approach to weight loss and improved health, author Ray Audette presents his groundbreaking "caveman" diet — an eating program that stems from the notion that what we ate before agriculture and technology evolved is still what our bodies need to function effectively, stave off disease, and stay lean and healthy. Read *NeaderThin* and you'll discover:

- How to become a modern-day Hunter-Gatherer and give up the addictive foods and habits that have kept you unhealthy and overweight.
- How a high-calorie, high-fat diet can actually make you leaner.
- Tips for getting started on the NeanderThin Diet, sticking with it, keeping a food diary, and more.
- Becoming Neander-Fit, a five-week exercise plan to complement your new diet.
- Dozens of delicious, easy-to-prepare NeanderThin recipes, including Chili, Cold Shrimp-Stuffed Avocados, Lemon Thyme Pesto Chicken, and Coconut Ice Cream.

THE EVOLUTION DIET: WHAT AND HOW WE WERE DESIGNED TO EAT

Written by
Joseph Stephen Breese Morse

D escription:

For two million years, humans evolved to eat a certain way: in the hunter/gatherer style, which consists of snacking on plant foods while roaming around before hunting and consequently filling themselves with animal meat. For the last few thousand years, however, our culture has forced us into a diet that is contrary to this. As a result, it is increasingly difficult to eat the way we were designed to eat. J.S.B. Morse's *Evolution Diet* explores this modern problem and how to adjust our diet to fix it. In the book, you'll find a thoughtful, often funny, survey of the make-up of the human body, contributing factors to our diet (such as culture), and an easy-to-grasp explanation of what exactly we should eat. You'll also find over 50 recipes for tasty Evolution Diet foods. This book will help you become

> "A man who strays from the path of understanding
> comes to rest in the company of the dead"
> (Prov. 21:16).

The World ⓥ The Word

the healthy and happy person you've always known you can be. It's time to evolve!"

Sounds fascinating; the only problem is, there never were any "cavemen"! Do you see how flawed ideas lead to more flawed ideas? I'm not a nutritional expert, but I do know that every diet idea under the sun has "had its day in the sun," so to speak. Who's to say that a "high calorie, high-fat diet" is healthy? What if it isn't? Do you see how this can be a problem, this evolutionary mindset? I've even read psychology studies that claim evils like rape are simply "leftovers" from our caveman, evolutionary past! Some modern science will justify anything!

It just goes to show you: be careful what you read; think critically before you adopt a world view.

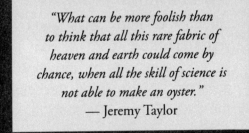

> "What can be more foolish than
> to think that all this rare fabric of
> heaven and earth could come by
> chance, when all the skill of science is
> not able to make an oyster."
> — Jeremy Taylor

103

THE HAPPIEST TODDLER ON THE BLOCK

Author
Harvey Karp, M.D.

Decades ago, before evolution theory was exploded like a bomb in the midst of the masses, the various theories were confined to laboratories (or seminaries, sadly enough). Yet in the past few years, these flawed theories have found their way into the mainstream. Get a load of the following goofy idea for communicating with a baby:

Description:

Toddlers can drive you bonkers . . . so adorable and fun one minute . . . so stubborn and demanding the next! Yet, as unbelievable as it sounds, there is a way to turn the daily stream of "nos" and "don'ts" into "yeses" and hugs — if you know how to speak your toddler's language. In one of the most useful advances in parenting techniques of the past 25 years, Dr. Karp reveals that toddlers, with their immature brains and stormy outbursts, should be thought of not as pint-size people, but as pint-size . . . cavemen. Having noticed that the usual techniques often failed to calm crying toddlers, Dr. Karp discovered that the key to effective communication was to speak to them in their own primitive language. When he did, suddenly he was able to soothe their outburst almost every time! This amazing success led him to the realization that children between the ages of one and four go through four stages of "evolutionary" growth, each linked to the development of the brain, and each echoing a step in prehistoric humankind's journey to civilization:

- "Charming Chimp-Child" (12 to 18 months): Wobbles around on two legs, grabs everything in reach, plays a nonstop game of "monkey see monkey do."

- "Knee-High Neanderthal" (18 to 24 months): Strong-willed, fun-loving, messy, with a vocabulary of about 30 words, the favorites being "no" and "mine."

- The "Clever Caveman" (24 to 36 months): Just beginning to learn how to share, make friends, take turns, and use the potty.

- The "Versatile Villager" (36 to 48 months): Loves to tell stories, sing songs, and dance, while trying hard to behave.

The stages-of-evolution theory has been thoroughly discredited in the scientific community; it was based on a series of phony illustrations cooked up by Ernst Haeckel, a German doctor in the 19th century. Haeckel so wanted Darwinian theory to be true that he manipulated the stages of a fetus to conform to the "animal to man" view. Although it's been debunked (even by evolutionists), you can see from the above description that it won't go gently into that good night. Thinking of your child as an advanced stage of evolution is downright sad. It also prevents you (and later, the child) from seeing him or her as a special creation of a loving God.

By the way, Dr. Karp is an assistant professor of pediatrics at UCLA. Does that scare anyone else?

> *"When God scooped up a handful of dust, and spit on it, and molded the shape of man, and blew a breath into it and told it to walk — that was a great day."*
> — Carl Sandburg

The World VS The Word

"The spirit of a man is the lamp of the LORD, searching all the inner depths of his heart" (Prov. 20:27).

WHERE DO WE GO FROM HERE?

For the weapons of our warfare are not carnal but mighty in God for pulling down strongholds, casting down arguments and every high thing that exalts itself against the knowledge of God, bringing every thought into captivity to the obedience of Christ (2 Cor. 10:4–5).

So, where do we go from here? Many of you may have been thinking as you went through all these examples that I spend all my time in front of the TV screen or at the movie theater. Not so! I've just been doing this talk for a long time now and the people who have been attending those meetings are sending me the examples that they're catching as they use their "radar."

The greatest compliment I receive is seeing folks *using* the culture to reach the lost or to train the next generation to be effective in sharing the gospel. It's exhilarating.

Our greatest desire is to see Christians get excited about their faith and start getting active in reaching the culture for Jesus Christ. In order for us to do this, though, we need to do some hard work.

The verse from Corinthians above tells us that there are "strongholds" that keep people from listening to the life-changing message of the gospel. If we're to be effective in sharing this vital message, we have to start pulling down those strongholds.

These strongholds can change in every generation. In our age, the message of "millions of years" and "evolution" truly are keeping many from ever believing that the Bible is truly the Word of God.

I tell folks all the time that our basic message really isn't about "creation vs. evolution." Ultimately, it's about "scriptural authority"! Can we really pick up the Bible and trust it from the very first verse?

Parents, you can use the examples that have been given to you in this book to now start training your children to deal with the false teachings of the world — to open up conversations showing that the Bible is relevant to today's culture.

I ask folks in church all the time, "Who knows more about dinosaurs, *Jurassic Park* or Jesus?" Overwhelmingly, these Christians will answer, "Jesus"! So I'll follow up with this question. "Then why is it when I ask a Christian a question about dinosaurs, 99 percent of them will give an answer with a *Jurassic Park* mentality?" If we're honest, it's because Jurassic Park has done more teaching on dinosaurs than church leaders using the Bible as real history.

No matter how "real" the dinosaurs on *Jurassic Park* look, if you want to know the truth about them you have to go to the only person who has always been there and KNOWS what it was like in the beginning. That person is God, who gave us a true history book, the Bible, so that we can KNOW what it was like in the beginning.

Friends, the world has been smart. They have a very focused message: Evolution is true — the millions of years of death and suffering is just a scientific fact. On the flip side, they teach us that the Bible is an old, outdated, irrelevant storybook.

Young person, do not be duped by the world. God's Word is true and trustworthy. It deals with the tough questions the world throws at us. We just have to allow it to be the foundation from which we start our thinking to get proper answers. As we talked about in the section on *Friends,* we need good, critical thinking skills to see the difference between "fact" and "fiction." Having a good understanding of the differences between "historical science" and "observational science" and solid answers to what we believe will help us to impact the culture.

Remember the movie *The Terminator?* In this 1984 action-filled movie, Arnold "The Governor" Schwarzenegger plays a cyborg that has been sent back from the future by evil machines to kill a woman who is supposedly going to give birth to a child that will lead a rebellion against those machines in the future.

This "terminator" is very single minded in its mission to kill this woman. It is programmed to see the world in a very unique, focused manner. You can see the computer working as they show you the world through the eyes of this cyborg. I call this "terminator vision."

Well, the world is very much like that. We all see the world in very specific ways, depending on how we've been programmed. We have to be aware of this programming if we want to break down the "strongholds" we spoke of earlier.

The same way that there is "terminator vision," there is "worldly vision"! Without recognizing this we will never succeed in reaching the real "lost world." By better understanding the strongholds, we can better understand what tools to use to overcome them.

If we are honest, the major tool that the church is using to evangelize the lost today is, "Jesus loves you and has a wonderful plan for your life!"

Please don't rush to judgment against me when I say this. I don't doubt this message at all. It is absolutely true, but there is more to our faith.

God commanded us to "Be diligent [study] to present yourself approved to God, a worker who does not need to be ashamed, rightly dividing the word of truth" (2 Tim. 2:15), and to "always be ready to give a defense to everyone who asks you a reason for the hope that is in you, with meekness and fear" (1 Pet. 3:15). When we aren't prepared to answer the questions that the world is asking, we are missing a huge opportunity to evangelize.

In order to break down the strongholds, we need to understand "worldly vision." The fact is that many see Christians in a very negative light. Bill Maher and Rosie O'Donnell teach the masses that we are "like Islamic terrorists" and that Christianity is a "mass-psychosis." In part, this is because many Christians are inconsistent with what they say they believe and aren't prepared to give that reasonable, rational explanation for why they believe.

Think about it. "Worldly vision" sees Christians as weak, intellectually inferior, and trusting an old, outdated book filled with fairy tales.

When they hear the "Jesus loves you" message, they don't understand it. Let's break it down.

"Jesus!" Who's that to you? Talk to ten different people and you'll get ten different interpretations of who He is. In addition, many times they look at us as if to say, "*You* don't believe the book you're telling me to trust, I can see it in your life, why should *I* trust it?"

"Loves You!" What's love? Think about what the world teaches as love. It most certainly doesn't line up with what the Word of God teaches. Without understanding God and what Christ did on the cross for everyone, they cannot understand love.

"Wonderful plan!" Unfortunately, "worldly vision" has trained the world to see everything through the lens of millions of years of death and suffering and evolution. Because of this training they say, "Are you kidding me? Look at the world around us! All I see is a world filled with millions of years of death and suffering. What kind of a loving God would allow such atrocities?"

"Your life!" In "worldly vision," this is the one thing that we get right. It is "my life" — Christian, don't impose your values and beliefs on me!

Can I suggest that we need more "Christian vision!" and this will only come when we start learning to *use* the culture, and not be *abused* by it. If we are to reach those folks, we need to be prepared. We have to understand the way that they see us and the way they hear what we are saying to them. We need to start mentoring/training programs across the globe teaching Christians how to deal with difficult issues, biblically.

We need to start answering the questions the world is asking, such as, "Where did Cain get his wife?" "Why would a loving God allow death and suffering?" "What about continental drift, carbon dating?" etc.

I recently spoke to a group of college students. This was not an AiG group, it was a diverse group of students from a variety of colleges, some secular, some Christian. Before I spoke, I asked them to take out a pencil and paper and write down the questions that they are being confronted with that are causing them to struggle with their faith. I was shocked. I asked them to do this before I spoke because I didn't want to influence them and I wanted to verify that our message is relevant today. I got back a stack of papers almost a quarter inch thick. All of the questions on that list were the ones that we deal with on our website and in our seminars. Every one of them!

Friends, we have to start reconnecting the Bible to the real world. By being obedient to God's Word and showing how to use it in our everyday life, something amazing happens. We actually start sharing the gospel of Christ.

My dear friend Mark Cahill said something to me a while back. He said, "Carl, evangelism is a conversation, not a presentation!" Mark is a guy that witnesses to every person he comes in contact with.

This really challenged me. We have to start conversing with those around us. Sometimes this is going to be difficult. My prayer is that the previous examples will make it easier for you to start "conversations" with the lost.

The reality is this — we only converse about things that we know about. Many of us can converse for a long time about sports, fishing, movies. . . . How about we start using what we see in the culture around us to turn those conversations to things that really matter.

Remember the "Terminator" example I gave. I always ask the folks at our seminars a couple of questions.

1. In the first *Terminator* movie, was Arnold a good guy or a bad guy? Everyone usually gets this right — a bad guy!
2. In the second *Terminator* movie, was Arnold a good guy or a bad guy? Everyone usually get this right as well — a good guy!

Then I ask, "What happened to change him?" Folks normally get this right. "He was 'reprogrammed!' " they say.

That's exactly what has to happen in the Church today. We have got to be "reprogrammed." George Barna made an interesting observation in one of his reports.

The vast majority of Christians do not behave differently because they do not think differently, and they do not think differently because we have never trained them, equipped them, or held them accountable to do so.*

Now, don't get me wrong. I'm not saying that we should watch movies or TV without doing our research. There are obvious limits to what believers should allow into their homes and into their hearts.

---

*George Barna, *The Second Coming of the Church: Blueprint for Survival* (Nashville, TN: Word, 1998), p. 122.

God's Word says:

I will behave wisely in a perfect way. . . . I will walk within my house with a perfect heart. I will set nothing wicked before my eyes (Ps. 101:2–3).

Thus saith the Lord, Learn not the way of the heathen, and be not dismayed at the signs of heaven; for the heathen are dismayed at them (Jer. 10:2; KJV).

Let's start training ourselves and the next generation to be effective in today's world. Daily Bible study and prayer have got to be a part of this retraining. May the Lord guide and direct your paths. God bless!

For more information, contact one of the Answers in Genesis ministries below. Answers in Genesis ministries are evangelical, Christ-centered, non-denominational, and non-profit.

Answers in Genesis
P.O. Box 510
Hebron, KY 41048
USA

Answers in Genesis
P.O. Box 8078
Leicester LE21 9AJ
United Kingdom

In addition, you may contact:

Institute for Creation Research
P.O. Box 2667
El Cajon, CA 92021

Coming Spring 2007...

creationmuseum

www.AnswersinGenesis.org

Also by Carl Kerby

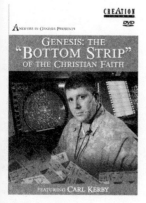

Genesis: "The Bottom Strip" of the Christian Faith

One of the world's most popular creation speakers, Carl Kerby uses creationism as an apologetic to explain the foundations found in Genesis. His engaging style holds up the Bible's first book as being critically important to doctrine and our everyday lives.

DVD • 49 minutes • 881994001965 • $12.99

Racism — Is There an Answer?

Millions worldwide are searching for answers to one of the greatest social challenges of our day. In this paradigm-changing DVD, Carl Kerby sheds light from God's Word and from real science on the truth about so-called "races" — we all share a common ancestor in Adam!

DVD • 45 minutes • 881994000562 • $12.99

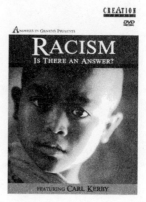

What Is the "Best" Evidence That God Created?

A favorite talk by one of AiG's most popular speakers! Audiences nationwide have been thrilled with this energetic eye-catching presentation on some of the most astounding evidences of God's handiwork. Carl Kerby builds to an unforgettable conclusion: the life-changing truth that the best evidence is God's Word itself!

DVD • 45 minutes • 881994000586 • $12.99